# MEXICO
## BEAUTIFUL LAND
## DIVERSE PEOPLE

# FAMOUS PEOPLE OF MEXICO

## ANNA CAREW-MILLER

The Mexican flag waves in the town square of Zocalo. The region that today is called Mexico has produced some of the most interesting figures in Western history.

# MEXICO
## BEAUTIFUL LAND
## DIVERSE PEOPLE

# FAMOUS PEOPLE
# OF MEXICO

## ANNA CAREW-MILLER

## Mason Crest Publishers
### Philadelphia

Produced by OTTN Publishing, Stockton, N.J.

**Mason Crest Publishers**
370 Reed Road
Broomall PA 19008
www.masoncrest.com

First Printing

1  3  5  7  9  8  6  4  2

Library of Congress Cataloging-in-Publication Data

Carew-Miller, Anna.
  Famous people of Mexico / Anna Carew Miller.
      p. cm. — (Mexico—beautiful land, diverse people)
  Includes index.
  ISBN 978-1-4222-0659-1 (hardcover) — ISBN 978-1-4222-
0726-0 (pbk.)
  1.  Mexico—Biography—Juvenile literature. [1.
Mexico—Biography.]  I. Title.
  CT553.C37 2008
  920.072—dc22
                                        2008031857

# TABLE OF CONTENTS

# MEXICO
## BEAUTIFUL LAND
## DIVERSE PEOPLE

# INTRODUCTION

exico is a country in the midst of great change. And what happens in Mexico reverberates in the United States, its neighbor to the north.

For outsiders, the most obvious of Mexico's recent changes has occurred in the political realm. From 1929 until the end of the 20th century, the country was ruled by a single political party: the Partido Revolucionario Institucional, or PRI (in English, the Institutional Revolutionary Party). Over the years, PRI governments became notorious for corruption, and the Mexican economy languished. In 2000, however, the PRI's stranglehold on national politics was broken with the election of Vicente Fox as Mexico's president. Fox, of the Partido de Acción Nacional (National Action Party), or PAN, promised political reform and economic development but had a mixed record as president. However, another PAN candidate, Felipe Calderón, succeeded Fox in 2006 after a hotly contested and highly controversial election. That election saw Calderón win by the slimmest of margins over a candidate from the Partido de la Revolución Democrática (Party of the Democratic Revolution). The days of one-party rule in Mexico, it seems, are gone for good.

Mexico's economy, like its politics, has seen significant changes in recent years. A 1994 free-trade agreement with the United States and Canada, along with the increasing transfer of industries from government control to private ownership under President Fox and President Calderón, has helped spur economic growth in Mexico. When all the world's countries are compared,

Mexico now falls into the upper-middle range in per-capita income. This means that, on average, Mexicans enjoy a higher standard of living than people in the majority of the world's countries. Yet averages can be misleading. In Mexico there is an enormous gap between haves and have-nots. According to some estimates, 40 percent of the country's more than 100 million people live in poverty. In some areas of Mexico, particularly in rural villages, jobs are almost nonexistent. This has driven millions of Mexicans to immigrate to the United States (with or without proper documentation) in search of a better life.

By 2006 more than 11 million people born in Mexico were living in the United States (including more than 6 million illegal immigrants), according to estimates based on data from the Pew Hispanic Center and the U.S. Census Bureau. Meanwhile, nearly one of every 10 people living in the United States was of Mexican ancestry. Clearly, Mexico and Mexicans have had—and will continue to have—a major influence on American society.

It is especially unfortunate, then, that many American students know little about their country's neighbor to the south. The books in the MEXICO: BEAUTIFUL LAND, DIVERSE PEOPLE series are designed to help correct that.

As readers will discover, Mexico boasts a rich, vibrant culture that is a blend of indigenous and European—especially Spanish—influences. More than 3,000 years ago, the Olmec people created a complex society and built imposing monuments that survive to this day in the Mexican states of Tabasco and Veracruz. In the fifth century A.D., when the Roman Empire collapsed and Europe entered its so-called Dark Age, the Mayan civilization was already flourishing in the jungles of the Yucatán Peninsula—and it would enjoy another four centuries of tremendous cultural achievements. By the time the Spanish conqueror Hernán Cortés landed at Veracruz in 1519, another great indigenous civilization, the Aztecs, had emerged to dominate much of Mexico.

With a force of about 500 soldiers, plus a few horses and cannons, Cortés marched inland toward the Aztec capital, Tenochtitlán. Built in the middle of a lake in what is now Mexico City, Tenochtitlán was an engineering marvel and one of the largest cities anywhere in the world at the time. With allies from among the indigenous peoples who resented being ruled by the Aztecs—and aided by a smallpox epidemic—Cortés and the Spaniards managed to conquer the Aztec Empire in 1521 after a brutal fight that devastated Tenochtitlán.

It was in that destruction that modern Mexico was born. Spaniards married indigenous people, creating mestizo offspring—as well as a distinctive Mexican culture that was neither Spanish nor indigenous but combined elements of both.

Spain ruled Mexico for three centuries. After an unsuccessful revolution in 1810, Mexico finally won its independence in 1821.

But the newly born country continued to face many difficulties. Among them were bad rulers, beginning with a military officer named Agustín Iturbide, who had himself crowned emperor only a year after Mexico threw off the yoke of Spain. In 1848 Mexico lost a war with the United States—and was forced to give up almost half of its territory as a result. During the 1860s French forces invaded Mexico and installed a puppet emperor. While Mexico regained its independence in 1867 under national hero Benito Juárez, the long dictatorship of Porfirio Díaz would soon follow.

Díaz was overthrown in a revolution that began in 1910, but Mexico would be racked by fighting until the Partido Revolucionario Institucional took over in 1929. The PRI brought stability and economic progress, but its rule became increasingly corrupt.

Today, with the PRI's long monopoly on power swept away, Mexico stands on the brink of a new era. Difficult problems such as entrenched inequalities and grinding poverty remain. But progress toward a more open political system may lead to economic and social progress as well. Mexico—a land with a rich and ancient heritage—may emerge as one of the 21st century's most inspiring success stories.

Montezuma II was one of the greatest rulers of ancient Mexico. As the ninth emperor of the Aztecs from 1502 until 1519, he created laws that pulled the empire together. It was his misfortune to be on the throne when Spanish soldiers under Hernán Cortés arrived.

# 1

# ANCIENT LEADERS

**B**efore the Spanish *conquistadors* set foot on the shores of Mexico, tribes of diverse native people had flourished there, including the Olmecs, the Toltecs, the Maya, and the Aztecs. The records that their sophisticated civilizations left behind tell of the accomplishments of great tribal leaders.

One such leader was Topiltzin Acxitl Quetzalcoatl, a 12th-century Toltec chieftain. Topiltzin was one of the last leaders of the powerful Toltec empire, which collapsed in the 12th century. The Aztecs, who thought of the Toltecs as their ancestors, revered Topiltzin as a god, and they kept his story alive.

Topiltzin's father was the ruler of the Toltec tribe, but he was assassinated when Topiltzin was a young man. Topiltzin avenged the murder and retook the throne, becoming the ruler of the Toltecs. He eliminated his enemies and focused his power in the city of Tula, the center of the Toltec empire.

Topiltzin was devoted to his belief in the peaceful god of knowledge, Quetzalcoatl. Eventually, he took on the name Quetzalcoatl, and the Aztecs believed he also assumed the powers of this kindly god.

However, Topiltzin Quetzalcoatl's kingdom was not peaceful. The forces that had led to his father's assassination continued to oppose him. Also, other tribes at the borders of the kingdom fought against his people. Because of this fighting, Topiltzin Quetzalcoatl was driven from his throne, never to return.

The Aztecs believed that Topiltzin Queztalcoatl disappeared in the east. In some versions of the story, he died but later appeared in the heavens as Venus, the morning star.

The Aztecs admired Topiltzin Queztalcoatl for his ability to control his kingdom through his wisdom and strength. These qualities were important to the Aztecs. Aztec records show that Itzcoatl, ruler of the Aztecs from 1427 to 1440, shared these qualities.

The Aztecs were a tribe of warriors who came from the north and settled in central Mexico, and Itzcoatl was an early founder of their empire. Because other tribes occupied much of the same territory, the Aztecs were forced to live on land no one else wanted, on a swampy island in the middle of Lake Texcoco. They claimed as their own the ancient city of Tenochtitlán, which was first settled in 1325.

During the reign of Itzcoatl, the original Aztec settlement began to be transformed into an amazing city. The Aztecs enlarged the small islands of the lake and created "floating gardens" from mud dredged from the lake bottom. The islands were connected to the shore by stone causeways, which had removable sections for defending the Aztec city.

The Aztecs were able to build Tenochtitlán's new splendor because Itzcoatl's leadership made it possible. He negotiated a treaty, which was

This native painting on cloth gives an idea of the size of Tenochtitlán, the Aztec capital. When the Spanish arrived in Mexico, Tenochtitlán was home to about 300,000 people, making it larger than any city of Europe at the time. Although the Aztecs had developed a complex government structure, a powerful military, a state religion, and an artistic tradition, Spanish conquistadors still viewed them as savages.

## TWO IMPORTANT GODS OF THE TOLTECS AND AZTECS:

*Quetzalcoatl* was the god of wind, light, and the morning star (Venus). He was also the god of knowledge and the founder of agriculture. Represented as a feathered serpent, he was a kind god, giving humans all the good aspects of civilization, including science, the calendar, and corn. Quetzalcoatl was worshipped by Mexican cultures more ancient than the Aztecs, including the Toltecs and the Mayas. He was considered to be the founder of the Toltec civilization. Sometimes Quetzalcoatl was depicted as a white man with a black beard. That's one of the reasons why Montezuma II believed that Cortés might have been Quetzalcoatl returning from the east.

The Aztecs believed the most powerful god was *Huitzilopoctli*, who was the god of the sun and war. In their belief system, Huitzilopoctli struggled with the forces of night to keep humans alive in the on-going battle between night and day. He needed the blood of human sacrifice to give him strength to fight his battle against the forces of night. He was a very important god to the Aztecs, because they believed that it was Huitzilopoctli who showed them where to build the city of Tenochtitlán.

called the Triple Alliance, with two other powerful tribes. Because the Aztecs had allies, they spent less time and money fighting off their enemies. Thanks to Itzcoatl's wisdom and diplomacy, the Aztecs had the time and the resources to build their great imperial center in the middle of Lake Texcoco.

Montezuma I was another great Aztec leader. He ruled from 1440 to 1468. Because he established the structure of the Aztec empire, he is considered the greatest of the Aztec rulers. During his reign, the city of Tenochtitlán was made even more beautiful and comfortable for its citizens, and his empire grew in size and wealth.

Montezuma I improved the city by having an *aqueduct*

AZTEC SERPENT FIGURE.

**Quetzalcoatl has been depicted in several forms, such as a feathered serpent (left) or a god emerging from the mouth of the earth (right). One of the most revered gods of the ancient Aztecs, tradition had it that Quetzalcoatl introduced maize, a vital crop to the people.**

built, which brought fresh water from the nearby mountains. He was responsible for creating a botanical garden with plants from all over his empire. He also enlarged the great pyramid in the center of the city by adding two temples at the top, one to Tlaloc, the rain god, and one to Huitzilopochtli, the god of war and the sun.

Montezuma I was able to pay for these improvements by sending out his warriors and forcing other tribes to submit to Aztec rule. He expanded the Atzec empire to the Gulf of Mexico to the east and to the Pacific in the south. The tribes that came within the domain of Montezuma I had to pay tribute, a tax for the protection of this powerful empire. From these other tribes in their territories, the Aztecs collected tribute of maize (corn), rubber, feathers, copper, and weapons. Prisoners of war were another kind of tribute that inspired great fear in the tribes, especially since these prisoners were sacrificed to Huitzilopochtli, the god of war. A man of great power, Montezuma I shaped an empire of beauty and terror for generations to come.

One of the last great leaders of the Aztecs was a descendant of the first Montezuma, Montezuma II, who ruled the Aztec empire from 1502 to 1520. Like his predecessors, he was not only a ruler but also a warrior and priest. He was called *huey tlatoani*, which means "great king" in the Aztec language.

Montezuma II is remembered for organizing the **bureaucracy** of his empire. He established stricter rules about social structure and controlled the outer boundaries of his empire. However, during his reign, the Triple Alliance, established by Itzcoatl, began to break down, so Montezuma II had to control many rebellions in his territories.

Montezuma II is also remembered for being the Aztec ruler who greeted the Spanish conquistador, Hernán Cortés, and his army at the entrance to the city of Tenochtitlán. Montezuma II had hesitated to send his warriors out to destroy Cortés. There had been omens that indicated to Montezuma that Cortés might be the god Quetzalcoatl, returning from the east. Montezuma II did not want to harm a god, but he did not trust these invaders.

Cortés took advantage of Montezuma's indecision. When Montezuma II invited Cortés and his men to be his guests in the city, Cortés took him hostage in his own palace. In the end, Montezuma II died as a prisoner of the Spanish conquistador, after he was hit in the head by a rock, thrown at him from a crowd of his own people who thought he had betrayed them to the Spanish conquerors. He died three days later, leaving his son, Cuauhtemoc, to lead the losing war against the Spanish.

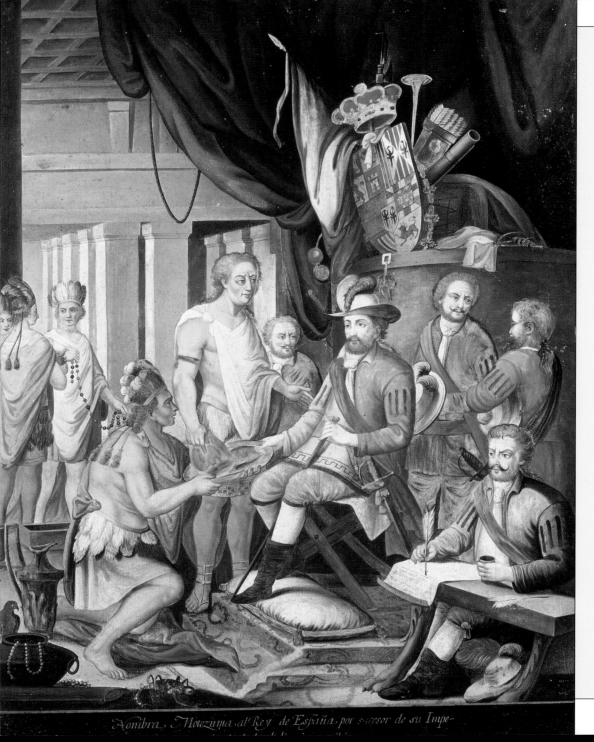

Nonibra Motezuma al Rey de España por sucesor de su Impe-

# 2

# CONQUERORS, SOLDIERS, AND REVOLUTIONARIES

The first European to have a great impact on the history of Mexico was Hernán Cortés. Looking back on their history, Mexicans disagree about whether Cortés was a hero or a villain, since he was the Spanish conquistador who overthrew the Aztec empire and won Mexico for the Spanish crown. While some say he brought the advantages of European civilization to Mexico, others say he is responsible for the near-destruction of Mexico's native civilizations.

Hernán Cortés was an aristocrat from Extremadura, a province in Spain that produced many other conquistadors. Although he originally went to

**One of the major events of Mexico's history was the meeting of the Aztec emperor Montezuma and the Spanish conquistador Hernán Cortés. In this painting by a Spanish artist, Montezuma kneels in a position of respect, offering gifts to Cortés.**

Española, then Cuba, he was given command of an *armada* to explore the mainland. When he landed in Yucatán, he found a shipwrecked Spaniard who spoke Mayan, the language of the tribe who lived there. This tribe gave him La Malinche (also called Doña Marina), a native woman who could speak both Mayan and the language of the Aztecs.

With their help as interpreters, Cortés moved inland, fighting and negotiating with the tribes he encountered. When he reached the Aztec city of Tenochtitlán, Montezuma II welcomed him. However, Cortés soon forced Montezuma II to acknowledge the Spanish king as his overlord.

After subduing the Aztec people of Tenochtitlán, Cortés destroyed the Aztec temples. The bloody rituals of human sacrifice shocked him, and he wanted to replace Aztec beliefs with Christianity. This angered the Aztecs. After Montezuma's death, his son Cuauhtemoc led his people's resistance against Cortés and his soldiers, but the superior weapons of the Spanish overpowered the Aztec warriors.

From the center of the Aztec empire, Cortés sent troops north, south, east, and west in order to subdue the rest of the country. However, conquering and controlling Mexico became the work of other representatives of the Spanish king, as Cortés was eventually sent back to Spain.

In spite of his accomplishments as a conquistador, Cortés did not end his life as a hero. Instead, he died a soldier's death in another Spanish military campaign in Africa. Although he was a Spaniard, Cortés asked to be buried in Mexico.

In the wake of Cortés, Mexico became a colony of Spain. Many people from Spain settled there in the hopes of making their fortune, and Mexico supplied Spain with the riches of its natural resources. For nearly 300 years, Spain controlled Mexico. In fact, no one born in Mexico could be part of its own government. Only men born in Spain could rule Mexico.

But in the 18th century, many people in Mexico felt it was time to rule themselves. Mexicans of European descent (called *criollos*), as well as those of mixed Indian and European descent (called *mestizos*) began to push for Mexican independence from Spain. One of these men was a landowner named Agustín de Iturbide.

At first, Iturbide was not on the side of independence. He was the son of a wealthy Spanish landowner and a Mexican mother. He became a soldier at age 17, first fighting against the rebels who wanted Mexican independence, including Miguel Hidalgo (who is discussed in a later chapter). After losing favor with the Royalists, who supported Spain, he retired. Worried about changes in Spanish politics that could affect Mexico, he later joined forces with the rebels, who wanted Mexico to be a modern democratic nation.

With his former enemies, he came up with the Plan de Iguala (1821), a plan for a new government in Mexico. This plan had three important ideas: independence from Spain, Catholicism

---

Iturbide was at his best as a warrior. In his memoirs, he wrote about how he felt about being in battle:

I was always happy during the war, victory was the inseparable companion of the troops I commanded. I did not lose one battle; I defeated as many enemy troops as attacked me or I encountered, even when they outnumbered me, as they often did, by ten to one.

The Plan of Iguala, a new system of government for Mexico, was the brainchild of Agustín de Iturbide. Iturbide soon became dictator of the country; this Mexican print shows him riding into Mexico City in triumph. However, he would rule Mexico for only a short period, until his repressive measures led to a revolt by Santa Anna. He was exiled in 1823; when he returned a year later, he was executed.

as the state religion, and equality of all races, including Indians, mestizos, and criollos. But when the Independence forces won under Iturbide's leadership, they disagreed about how to form a new government.

In the confusion of 1822, Iturbide was proclaimed "Emperor of Mexico" by **conservative** military forces. Unfortunately, Iturbide was a better soldier than politician. Even though the economy was ruined by the war, he wanted to rule with the style and luxury of a king, ignoring the democratic goals of his former allies. By end of the year, he had broken up the new congress and proclaimed himself dictator. Rebel forces soon overwhelmed him. In 1823, he stepped down and left Mexico.

Because Iturbide felt that Mexico needed him, he returned from **exile** in Europe in 1824 to reclaim the throne. Soon after arriving on Mexico's shore, he was executed by those who had opposed his dictatorship.

The man who led the forces that defeated Iturbide was Antonio López de Santa Anna. As an army officer and statesman, he was leader of Mexico between 1833 and 1855, 11 different times. He was considered a brave military leader and a wily politician, a

**Antonio López de Santa Anna was leader of Mexico on 11 different occasions. He was considered a brave military leader but a ruthless politician.**

24

In the United States, Santa Anna is remembered for his role in the history of Texas. In 1835, he marched on an American colony in Texas, which was then part of Mexico. These settlers had rebelled against Mexican authority, even though they had agreed to abide by Mexican laws when they asked to colonize this northern part of Mexico. Santa Anna's forces killed all the defenders of the fort at the Alamo. Revenge for this loss motivated Texan soldiers who cried, "Remember the Alamo" during the battle of San Jacinto six weeks later, at which Texas won its freedom.

courageous hero and a power-hungry villain.

Santa Anna's abilities as a military leader were important in the turbulent years that followed the Mexican War of Independence. Because Mexico had borrowed money from other countries to fight its war, it had many debts to pay afterward. It could not repay those debts easily because so much of the country had been destroyed in the fighting. But France and the United States, who had loaned Mexico money, were determined to have the money repaid. Led by Santa Anna, Mexico went to war with France and then the United States because of these debts.

Santa Anna used his military success to gain political power. After successfully driving French forces out, he became dictator of Mexico. He lost his position and was exiled to Cuba, but he returned to fight against American forces in the Mexican-American War of 1846. Many Mexicans still blame Santa Anna for losing this war and negotiating away half Mexico's territories to the United States.

In spite of this failure, Santa Anna returned to power several more times. His last chance at running the country came in 1853, when the Mexican congress's conservative leaders asked him to be king of Mexico. He was soon overthrown by liberal forces and went into final

**Pancho Villa (second from left) and Emiliano Zapata (third from left), two of the most important leaders of Mexico during the early 20th century, are seated at the center of this photograph. Villa and Zapata are flanked by two fellow revolutionaries, Tomás Urbina and Otilio Montaño.**

exile in 1855.

At the beginning of the 20th century, Mexico was ready for another revolution, this time a revolution whose goals were to create a more democratic society. One of the best-known warriors of the Revolution was Emiliano Zapata. He was a passionate leader of Indian descent from the southern state of Morelos.

He organized the Indian and mestizo people in the south to fight for a chance to farm their own land instead of working for the rich landowners. His motto was "Tierra y Libertad" (Land and Freedom). He led guerilla troops in the south during the years of the revolution, but military victory was not enough; he wanted reform.

At first, Zapata's troops, called *zapatistas*, fought alongside the most powerful group of revolutionary forces. When this **moderate** group finally seized power, Zapata decided to fight against them, too. After meeting with their leader, Francisco Madero, Zapata realized that land reform was not a priority of the new government.

In spite of the chaotic situation in Mexico during the years of the Revolution, Zapata controlled his home state. In Morelos, Zapata put his program for land reform, called the Plan de Ayala, into effect. His followers could put down their weapons and take up their tools for farming. Unfortunately, he never lived to see the rewards of his leadership. Zapata was **ambushed** by

Traditional wars were fought by well-armed soldiers, who faced each other on battlefields. Zapata could not fight this way because his soldiers did not have weapons as powerful as those of the government's armies. So he became a *guerilla*, fighting in surprise attacks, often at night and with small groups of soldiers.

government soldiers and killed in 1919.

Like Emiliano Zapata, Pancho Villa was a guerilla leader of the Mexican Revolution, but he fought in the northern state of Chihuahua. Unlike Zapata, Villa had been on the wrong side of the law before the Revolution, having joined a gang of bandits when he was 17. Although Villa had settled down, married, and opened a butcher's shop, he picked up his guns once again in 1910. He decided to become a soldier for the landowners who supported the revolution.

In the 10 years of *civil* war, he used what he had learned as a bandit to become a military strategist and a leader of the revolutionary armies of northern Mexico. Because he had conflicts with Victoriano Huerta, the commander-in-chief of the republican forces, he was imprisoned in 1912, but he escaped to Texas.

> Villa was considered a hero by many, a bandit by others, a sort of Mexican Robin Hood. His bravery and charisma were celebrated in corridos (popular folk songs). Here is one verse from a corrido about Villa:
>
> *Get ready now, federales*
> *[the government's army],*
> *Be prepared for very hard rides,*
> *For Villa and his soldiers*
> *Will soon take off your hides.*

After the old government fell and the new government took over, Villa met with Zapata. They agreed to keep fighting the new government. They didn't believe that the new government would be much better than the old one for people like them, who never had much money or power. Unlike Zapata, Villa survived the Revolution and retired, but he was killed in a mysterious attack in 1923.

The statue of Father Miguel Hidalgo stands in a village plaza. On the day after Independence Day throughout Mexico, statues of the padre are decorated with flowers to honor his role in winning Mexico's freedom from Spain.

# THE POLITICIANS AND SHAPERS OF A NATION

**M**iguel Hidalgo was a Catholic priest from Spain who is remembered as the father of Mexican independence. He was born to wealthy *criollo* parents in Guanajuato, where he studied to be a priest and teacher. Later, he was dismissed from his teaching post because of his **liberal** ideas and behavior. But he was beloved by the Indians who were his parishioners in the village of Dolores.

In the years before the War of Independence, Hidalgo became the leader of a literary club that did more than read books. They plotted for Mexican independence. When their plot was discovered, Hidalgo decided to begin his revolution, even though he was not prepared. The fight for Mexican independence began in 1810 when Hidalgo issued the

**30**

*Grito de Dolores* (Cry of Dolores), which demanded freedom for all Mexicans and an end to bad government.

Hidalgo's message appealed to the lower levels of Mexican society, the **peasants**, workers, and Indians who wanted revenge for social, economic, and racial injustice. However, Hidalgo couldn't control the violence of his followers, whose cry was "Death to the *gachupines* (Spanish-born Mexicans)".

The government fought back harshly and successfully. Six months later, Hidalgo was captured and executed. He had led only with ideas. He didn't have a real political or military strategy, other than to rid Mexico of the old order in order to create a new, more just order. Mexico's War of Independence had to wait for other leaders.

One of the most beloved figures in Mexican history is Benito Juárez, a hero and president who fought to establish a democratic government. Juárez was born into a Zapotec Indian family but became an orphan at an early age. Fortunately, a benefactor paid for his education to become a priest. Instead, he studied law and became a politician.

After serving in the state and national legislature, Juárez became governor of his native state of Oaxaca in 1848. However, Santa Anna forced him from Mexico because of his liberal ideas. In 1855, he returned and fought

Hidalgo's passion for justice in Mexico can be heard in the words of his last sermon, given to the Indians of Saltillo:

"...I have come from the south, from making war on the Spaniards in order to tear the country out of their hands, for it does not belong to them and they have held it for a long time with cruelty and tyranny and grave damage to the original inhabitants, the children of the nation..."

Born to Zapotec parents in Oaxaca, Benito Pablo Juárez went on to become Mexico's president twice. His birthday is now a national holiday across the country.

32

The tumultuous political climate of Mexico in the early 20th century meant that no ruler stayed in power for very long. Francisco Indalecio Madero managed to wrest the presidency away from Porfirio Díaz, but was overthrown himself after only two years.

against Santa Anna's regime, eventually becoming minister of justice under a new, more democratic president.

One of his most important acts was to write the *Ley* (law) *Juárez*, which took away power from the rich and powerful Catholic Church and the military and gave legal authority to the **civilian** government. He also helped to write the new constitution of Mexico in 1857.

Juárez was part of a government that made many changes, too many for some Mexicans. Conservative factions tried to take control of government in the costly War of Reform. Then, they conspired with the French to bring in Archduke Maximilian from Austria to be emperor of Mexico. Forced to leave Mexico again, Juárez continued to lead the liberal government. Its forces resisted and eventually got rid of the foreign emperor.

Because he was considered so just and wise, Juárez was elected president four times. He died in office in 1872. He is remembered as a great leader because he rose to power as an Indian in a prejudiced society and maintained his power as a civilian in a time of military power.

Porfirio Díaz was another powerful Mexican leader, a great soldier who became president of Mexico. He established a strong centralized government, which he dominated for more than 30 years.

Born into a hard-working *mestizo* family in Oaxaca, Díaz did not have any easy childhood. Like Benito Juárez, he studied first for the priesthood and then law, but he didn't finish either course of studies. Instead, he entered the military to aid the liberal cause. As a young brigadier general, Díaz defeated the French invaders on May 5, 1862 (which is celebrated as *Cinco de Mayo*, an important Mexican holiday). Later, Díaz began his political career as a member of the Mexican congress.

Because he disagreed with Benito Juárez and his supporters who were his former allies, Díaz took control of the presidency by force in 1877. His 34 years in power are called the Porfiriato. During his regime, Díaz built up the rural police force and gave the Catholic Church back some of the power it lost during the period of reform. He made more land available to wealthy landowners, which left less land for Native Americans and peasants.

While the lives of the poor did not improve under Díaz's leadership, his policies did allow Mexico to become a more modern industrial country. This progress included the growth of railroads, industry, and mining. But all of this did little to help the living conditions of those at the bottom of the social ladder.

By the end of Díaz's regime, many Mexican people wanted a change. They wanted a government that would address the social and economic injustices of Mexican society. In the midst of the violence of the Revolution, Díaz was forced to resign. He spent the last four years of his life in exile in Europe.

After Díaz's fall from power, Francisco Madero became an unlikely leader of the Mexican Revolution; he was also, briefly, Mexico's president who tried to reform the old government. He

**THE CONSTITUTION OF 1857**

Mexico's new constitution created many laws in order to form a modern, democratic nation. It established a legislature, gave the right to vote to all men over 21, and abolished all forms of slavery and titles of nobility. It included a bill of rights, which provided freedoms of speech, press, assembly, and education.

was a wealthy, thoughtful man who became known as "the apostle of democracy."

Madero began his political career by getting involved in local politics and writing for newspapers. He didn't like what Díaz was doing to Mexico, and he wanted a return to the ideals of the 1857 constitution. Madero did not want a revolution, and he hoped for a peaceful, democratic change.

In 1910, Madero became a presidential candidate opposing Díaz. But he was imprisoned by President Díaz during the election and lost. While in prison, he came up with the Plan of San Luis Potosí. Madero's plan declared that the election was a fraud and that he would act as president until new elections. The plan also called for an uprising, but Díaz suppressed the revolutionary agitators.

In spite of Díaz's actions, the Revolution began anyway, forcing Díaz to resign. Although Madero was the leader, he couldn't control the various *radical* and conservative components of the Revolution. His ideas were too moderate for both sides. In 1912, Madero was forced to resign at the hands of his own military leaders, and was fatally shot 10 days later while he was being transported to prison.

Lázaro Cárdenas was president of Mexico from 1934 to 1940. He is best known for trying to carry out the goals of the Revolution. Born in Michoacán to a middle-class family, he joined the Zapata's Revolution at the age of 18. By 25, he was a general for the government's forces fighting against Zapata. Then he supported the revolt against President Venustiano Carranza, because he thought that Carranza's government was corrupt and not interested in furthering the goals of the Revolution.

36

After gaining political experience as a governor and leader of his political party, Cárdenas became president. Unlike Madero, he had the support of radical groups, those people who had been most critical of the government during the Revolution and afterward. They trusted him because of his *progressive* views and because he was known for being honest and sincere.

Vicente Fox served as president of Mexico from 2000 to 2006. During his administration, the Mexican economy did not grow as quickly as he had hoped. Still, under Fox, the country's governmental accountability and standard of living improved in many ways.

Cárdenas had a Six-Year Plan, which restored much of the power to labor unions, united peasant organizations, redistributed over 40 million acres of land, and created a credit union for those working on *ejidos* (communal farms). Also, he nationalized the petroleum industry, which upset foreign petroleum owners in the United States and Britain. Finally, he vigorously promoted tourism, celebrating Mexico's rich heritage. Cárdenas remained a presence in Mexican politics until his death in 1970.

In 2000, Vicente Fox became the first Mexican president to be elected since the Revolution who was not a member of the Party of the Institutionalized Revolution. Before going into politics, Fox was an executive for Coca-Cola and an independent rancher. He joined the conservative National Action Party (PAN) in 1988 and became governor of Guanajuato from 1994 to 1999. As president, Fox's main goals were to improve the educational system, increase political accountability, and allow business and industry to expand the economy with less government interference.

Whether or not they agreed with Fox's views, most Mexicans saw Fox's election as a sign of Mexico's progress towards becoming a more democratic country, no longer dominated by one political party. After midterm elections in 2003, no party captured a majority of representatives, suggesting that the multi-party system has the potential to last. In 2006, Felipe Calderón, also a member of PAN, succeeded Fox in a very close presidential election. Although the results were controversial and required recounts, the peaceful transfer of power was a positive sign for fair, representative democracy.

A pedestrian walks past the enormous sculpted heads of three 19th-century Mexican patriots—Benito Juárez, Miguel Hidalgo y Costilla, and Venustiano Carranza—in Ensenada, Baja California.

# MEXICO'S GREAT THINKERS AND INTELLECTUALS

**M**any citizens who were not politicians or soldiers shaped the destiny of Mexico. One such Mexican is José Joaquín Fernández de Lizardi, who is remembered as a leading figure of the movement to liberate Mexico from Spain. He was a novelist, a journalist, and a political activist at a time when Mexico was defining itself as an independent nation.

Lizardi was born in Mexico City and began studying theology when he was 17. But, like many other famous Mexicans, he chose to go into government service instead of becoming a priest. When the struggle for independence began in 1810, he was a judge in Acapulco. He left politics to start a newspaper called *El Pensador Mexicano* (The Mexican Thinker). In his writing, he used ***satire*** to promote change, but his ideas often made him end up in prison.

When he was imprisoned for writing about his views, he wrote what is considered Mexico's first novel, the title of which is translated as *The Itching Parrot* (1816). Lizardi believed that reading and writing were important forces that could help change Mexico into an independent republic, so he founded the Public Society of Reading in 1820, which distributed books and newspapers. Lizardi's contribution to the intellectual life of Mexico encouraged the fight for independence and the creation of the new Mexican nation in the early 19th century.

Another Mexican intellectual who influenced the politics of Mexico but who was not a politician was Ricardo Flores Magón, a radical thinker whose ideas helped to bring about the Mexican Revolution of 1910. Magón began his life as a radical in 1890, when he was imprisoned for following a student protest against Díaz's government. In 1900, with his brothers, he started *Regeneración (Regeneration)*, an opposition newspaper, which criticized Díaz for bringing progress to Mexico at too high a cost to workers and farm laborers. Together, the Magón brothers began what were called "Liberal Clubs," *anarchist* groups that inspired the ideas of the Revolution, especially ideas about the rights of workers and peasants.

After being imprisoned several times, the Magón brothers went to the United States, where they published *Regeneración* and sent it to workers in Mexico. By 1906, even though it was too dangerous for him to live in Mexico, Ricardo Magón became the leader of a new political party, the Liberal Mexican Party (PLM).

Magón's radical ideas made him many enemies in Mexico and the United States. In 1907, President Díaz persuaded the U.S. government to

Although Porfirio Díaz (pictured) ruled Mexico for 34 years, his policies were not always popular with the common man. Although it was often dangerous for them to do so, revolutionaries such as Ricardo Flores Magón spoke out against the politics of the day.

arrest Magón for encouraging workers to go on strike in Mexican factories. After being imprisoned in the United States several times, Magón was finally charged with espionage and sentenced to 20 years in jail. He died in a Kansas prison in 1916.

Not all great Mexican intellectuals were interested in revolution, however. Alfonso Reyes was a writer, educator, and diplomat. Never a revolutionary or politician, Reyes made his mark as a thoughtful scholar and thinker.

Reyes began his career writing sophisticated literary criticism while he was still a student. But rather than become a teacher, he went on to receive a law degree. Reyes stayed away from Mexico during the chaotic years that followed the Revolution. Beginning in 1913, he worked for the government as a diplomat, first in Europe, then in Latin America. During his diplomatic career, he continued to write scholarly work but also produced creative pieces, including poetry. As a scholar, he specialized in classical Greek literature and Spanish literature. His creative writing did not reflect the passionate politics of Mexico, but it was still widely respected.

Agustín Yáñez (pictured) was appointed secretary of education under Mexico's President Gustavo Díaz Ordaz in 1968. Though Díaz Ordaz's term was successful economically, he became unpopular after he ordered the massacre of student and labor demonstrators that same year. Yáñez was criticized for his refusal to step down from office in protest or make a statement regarding the government's violent act of repression.

When he retired as a diplomat, Reyes devoted himself to education and scholarship until the end of his career. Under President Cárdenas, he was the director of the *Casa de España*, a school for refugees of the Spanish Civil War. This school later became a famous school of higher education, *El Colegio de México*.

A man of many talents, Agustín Yáñez had a career similar to his predecessor, Alfonso Reyes. Like Reyes, he began his career as a scholar and diplomat, but he became more actively involved in politics than Reyes ever did. However, Yáñez is remembered more for his work as a writer and journalist than as a statesman and politician.

Yáñez's gifts as a student emerged early, and he began teaching when he was only 15, soon becoming a professor at the National University. He began his political career as a diplomat, then became involved in local politics and served as governor of the state of Jalisco from 1953 to 1959.

**Rooftops glisten in the afternoon sun in Puerto Vallarta, Jalisco. Journalist and writer Agustín Yáñez governed this seaside state for six years.**

The most challenging time of Yáñez's political career occurred in 1968, when he was secretary of education in the *cabinet* of President Gustavo Díaz Ordaz. During the late 1960s, Mexico, like much of Europe and the United States, experienced the turmoil and passion of a student movement. Young people publicly demonstrated to show their dissatisfaction with their leaders. In 1968, police and government soldiers fired on a crowd of student protestors at Tlatelolco Plaza in Mexico City, killing many of them and creating a huge crisis. As secretary of education, Yáñez was important in starting a dialogue between the leaders of the student movement and the government. This dialogue prevented further violence.

In addition to his career in politics, Yáñez worked steadily as a writer. He edited three journals and wrote two well-known novels, *Al Filo del Agua (The Edge of the Storm)* in 1947 and *Las Tierras Flacas (The Lean Lands)* in 1963.

Diego Rivera was one of the most important and well-known painters of 20th century Mexico. Rivera's work can be seen all over Mexico, not only in museums but also painted on the walls, inside or out, of many public buildings.

# ARTISTS AND WRITERS

**M**any creative Mexicans contributed to the identity of Mexico through their work. The previous chapter discussed several writers whose ideas shaped Mexico. In this chapter, each artist or writer contributed not only to the shape of Mexican culture but also to the creative field in which he worked.

Manuel Gutiérrez Nájera is an important Mexican poet. He is given credit for connecting Mexican literature to the international ideas of **Modernism**. As a poet, Gutiérrez Nájera attempted to give new life to the language of Spanish poetry and abandoned older Mexican forms in favor of new ideas that came from France. Like other Modernists, Gutiérrez Nájera wanted his writing to express the loneliness and isolation of modern urban life, and his poetry was elegant and somber. While some critics thought that Gutiérrez Nájera's work wasn't Mexican enough, others considered him one of the best of Mexico's poets.

In addition to writing poetry, Gutiérrez Nájera encouraged the work of other poets in his literary journal, *Revista Azul (Blue Review)*, which

**46**

published the poetry of many young Mexican writers. Sadly, Gutiérrez Nájera died from complications of alcoholism at the age of 36.

One of the most famous figures in Mexico's history is Diego Rivera, a painter who revived the art of large-scale murals and who had a huge impact on the international art world. Rivera began his life as an artist at Mexico's Academy of Fine Arts, where he studied from 1898 to 1906. With a government fellowship, he then studied art in Europe, where he was especially fascinated by the frescoes of Renaissance Italy. Rivera lived in Paris and was friends with many great painters, including Pablo Picasso and Henri Matisse. Their new ways of painting and seeing the world had a great influence on him.

Although Rivera was in Europe during the years of the Mexican Revolution, his work was motivated by political ideas. He wanted to bring public art to all the people, not just those who could afford to buy it. Because he was interested in Mexico's native heritage, he combined modern European styles with themes from Mexican history, both ancient and modern.

In the 1930s, Rivera, along with José Clemente Orozco and David Alfaro Siqueiros, started creating murals, putting their large-scale paintings on the walls of public buildings. Rivera's first project was at the National Preparatory School, where his murals created controversy with their political subjects. Not everyone was interested in public art that spoke out against oppression and represented Mexico's

**Frescoes are a kind of large-scale painting in which the artist paints on the wet plaster of a wall instead of a canvas. The ceiling of the Sistine Chapel in Rome is covered with the frescoes of Michaelangelo, the Renaissance artist.**

native heritage.

Rivera had a passionate personality. Conflict was part of his life as an artist as well as his personal life. He was married several times, twice to Frida Kahlo, who was also a famous artist.

Like Rivera, Octavio Paz was fascinated by his country's history and by the struggles of its common people. Paz, however, was not a painter but an important Mexican writer who won a Nobel Prize in 1990. His work, with its focus on identity issues in a complex and often conflicted culture, has influenced contemporary Latin American writing.

Paz was born in Mexico City in 1914 into a family that cared about books and

**One of the most articulate voices of Mexico is Octavio Paz (left), shown receiving the Nobel Prize for his poetry in 1990. His work is important to the Mexican people because much of it is directed toward the country's political and historical issues.**

Not only a novelist but also a political analyst of sorts, Carlos Fuentes has written both about the Mexican and American government systems. Although he has spent much of his life in Mexico, he was raised in Washington, D.C., and visits the United States often.

ideas. His father was a lawyer who had supported Zapata during the Revolution, and his grandfather had an unusually large library, which Paz read as a child. After studying in Mexico, he went to the United States to study Hispanic poetry.

Paz traveled as a writer, going to Spain during the Spanish Civil War and, in 1944, to New York to study Spanish American poetry. In 1945, he became a diplomat, serving at posts in Europe, Japan, and India. In 1968, when he heard about the massacre of the student protesters in Tlatelolco Plaza, he resigned his post. He compared the terrible event to the Aztec ritual sacrifices in which those in power used violence to keep order.

In his most famous book, *The Labyrinth of Solitude* (1950), Paz analyzed what it means to be Mexican. As in much of his other work, he explored Mexican history and its influence on the Mexican way of thinking. Throughout his life and work, Paz opposed injustice and the violations of human rights.

Carlos Fuentes is another Mexican writer and also a playwright whose experimental style has brought him international praise. Like Paz, much of his writing focuses on the connections between the individual Mexican and the complex history of Mexico.

Perhaps the question of what it means to be Mexican was important to Fuentes because he spent the early part of his life outside of Mexico. His father was a diplomat, so he was born in Panama and lived in many other countries before his family returned to Mexico when he was 16.

Similar to Octavio Paz, Fuentes became a diplomat in the 1950s, after receiving a law degree from Mexico's National Autonomous University. From that time on, Fuentes balanced parallel careers in writing and government service. In the 1950s, he started a literary magazine, and he worked as the director of international cultural relations. Like Paz, Fuentes spoke out against the Tlatelolco student massacre in 1968.

Of his 11 novels, one of the best known is *The Death of Artemio Cruz* (1962), which follows the life of one man but really is about how Mexico never achieved the goals of the Revolution. Fuentes has received many important awards for his literary work, and his writing is widely translated.

# MEXICO'S EXTRAORDINARY WOMEN

**F**or her role in Cortés's conquest of Mexico, La Malinche is considered by some to be an example of a courageous intelligent woman and by others to be a traitor who betrayed her native people to the Spanish conquerors. The daughter of a native nobleman, she had been traded as a slave to another tribe. When Cortés came upon this tribe, she

**Nahuatl is still spoken by over one million Mexicans.**

was given to him as a gift and was named Doña Marina. Because she could speak both Mayan and Nahuatl (the language of the Aztecs), she became Cortés's interpreter and companion.

**La Malinche (also known as Doña Marina) interprets for Cortés during a meeting with Aztec emmissaries. A former slave who was given to Cortés by one of the tribes he encountered in Mexico, she was an important part of the Spanish success in conquering the Aztecs.**

**52**

Doña Marina was from a tribe that had been oppressed by the Aztecs, which may be why she was willing to help the Spaniards with their conquest. She was more than an interpreter, for she gave advice to both Cortés and each Indian community they encountered, helping the native people decide whether to fight Cortés or join him. Her intelligence saved Cortés and his men from several dangerous situations, and she demonstrated her courage by risking her life alongside his soldiers.

Eventually, Doña Marina had a son with Cortés, who was named Martín, after Cortés's father. Before Cortés left Mexico permanently, he granted her land near the conquered Aztec city of Tenochtitlán, where she established a home with her children and husband, another Spanish soldier.

One of the greatest poets and thinkers of colonial Mexico was also a woman, Sor Juana Inés de la Cruz. She was born in a village outside Mexico City, the illegitimate child of a Basque captain and a *criollo* woman. As a precocious child, she wrote her first poem at the age of eight and could read and write Latin. Her extraordinary intellect impressed the nobles in the court of the Spanish viceroy, Mexico's ruler.

She joined the Convent of St. Jerome as a teenager in order to devote herself to an intellectual life, something she felt she could not do if she were to marry.

As a nun, Sor Juana wrote plays, essays, and poetry, and she had a famous large library of 4,000 books. The subject of her writing was often the position and

**Here is a translation of one of Sor Juana's poems about the unfairness of men towards women.**

*Stupid men, quick to condemn*
*Women wrongly for their flaws,*
*Never seeing you're the cause*
*Of all that you blame in them!*

**Sor Juana Inés de la Cruz is one of the most recognized historical figures in Mexico. Her striking literary assertions about gender roles and misconceptions are as pointed and challenging today as they were in the 17th century.**

treatment of women. Sor Juana was criticized for wanting to do more than study religious topics. When she was 42, she gave up all her work except her religious studies and sold her books. She died soon afterward during an *epidemic*.

Unlike Sor Juana, Empress Carlota was not truly a Mexican woman but a Belgian princess who became the wife of Emperor Maximilian. A strong personality, she was considered the power behind the throne. Maximilian and Carlota came to Mexico in 1864 as part of the plot of conservative Mexicans and Emperor Napoleon of France. The conservatives thought that they could control Maximilian to regain their power, and meanwhile, Napoleon hoped to have a foothold for his French empire. However,

**Empress Carlota of Mexico was actually a Belgian princess. She married the Archduke of Austria, who became emperor of Mexico in 1864, but their reign would last only a few years. She spent the last years of her life being treated for mental illness.**

Maximilian didn't do what the conservative Mexicans wanted. Instead, with the support and encouragement of Carlota, he tried to improve conditions in Mexico.

As an outsider in Mexico, Maximilian needed the backing of Napoleon. After the end of the American Civil War, Napoleon foresaw problems with the United States, who didn't want French imperial interests so close to their borders. He withdrew support from Maximilian.

In 1866, Carlota predicted disaster for her husband, so she went to Europe to beg for assistance. After Napoleon refused to keep his original promises to support Maximilian, she wrote to her husband that Napoleon was "quite the devil in person." Carlota did not succeed in her quest for help. On her way to ask for the Pope's help in Rome, she showed the first signs of mental illness. She was taken to Belgium, where she lived out the remainder of her life insane, never knowing that her husband had been executed by Juárez's forces.

Not all women involved in Mexican politics did so at their husbands' sides. Brave and independent, Juana Belén Gutiérrez de Mendoza was a political writer and activist who spoke for the common people during the Mexican Revolution.

Born into a hard-working family in Durango in 1880, she joined the critics of Porfirio Díaz when she was only 21. Although her first published writing was a book of poetry, her most influential work was what she wrote for the newspaper she helped to found. In her newspaper writing, she not only criticized the government but also called on the Mexican people to be more courageous in opposing Díaz.

In 1904, Gutiérrez de Mendoza's passionate writing landed her in prison, where she stayed for three years. When she was released, she joined the followers of Zapata, in the hopes of creating a democratic Mexico. Even after Zapata's death and the disappointments of the government that followed the Revolution, Gutiérrez de Mendoza continued to write about and work for her democratic ideals.

A different type of artist, Frida Kahlo was a painter whose colorful and highly personal style of painting brought her international fame. The

Frida Kahlo's unique artistic vision of her world and herself was fostered by her experiences in Mexico, her relationship with Diego Rivera, and her, at times intense, physical pain due to an accident. Much of her artwork expresses her tormented mental state.

daughter of a German Jewish photographer and his Mexican wife, Kahlo was one of the first women to attend the National Preparatory School.

After a traffic accident in 1924 that fractured her pelvis and shattered her right leg and foot, Kahlo left school and took up painting. She met the muralist, Diego Rivera, who recognized her talent and encouraged her work. In 1929, Kahlo married Rivera.

Kahlo found the subjects for her work in her life. Her paintings often focused on her relationship to Rivera and her lifelong pain as a result of the accident. Even so, her identity as a Mexican was essential to her work, and her paintings have many references to Mexico's history and native cultures.

Because the subject of her work was often strange or dreamlike, art critics labeled Frida Kahlo as a Surrealist, which meant that her work was about the subconscious mind or dreams. Kahlo disagreed. She said: "They thought I was a Surrealist but I wasn't. I never painted dreams. I painted my reality."

These women, from La Malinche to Kahlo, like other famous Mexicans, used their strong personalities and rich heritage to help build a better Mexico.

## CHRONOLOGY

| | |
|---|---|
| **12th century** | Topiltzin rules the Toltecs. |
| **1325** | The city of Tenochtitlán is built. |
| **1427-1440** | Under Itzcoatl, the Aztecs expand their empire. |
| **1440-1468** | Under Montezuma I, the Aztecs' power grows still greater. |
| **1502** | Montezuma II becomes emperor of the Aztecs. |
| **1519** | Cortés arrives in Mexico and begins his conquest. |
| **1810** | Miguel Hidalgo y Castilla begins the War of Independence against Spain. |
| **1821** | Agustín de Iturbide successfully leads Mexican forces to Independence against Spain. |
| **1822-1823** | Agustín de Iturbide is "Emperor of Mexico." |
| **1833** | Santa Anna becomes president for the first of 11 times. |
| **1846-1848** | War between Mexico and the United States, in which Mexico is defeated and loses half its territory to the United States. |
| **1855** | Santa Anna is overthrown by liberal forces. |
| **1857** | Mexico has a new and liberal constitution. |
| **1858-1861** | The War of Reform is fought between conservative forces and liberal forces, led by Benito Juárez. |
| **1864** | Maximilian, Archduke of Austria, is crowned Emperor of Mexico. |
| **1867** | Liberal armies defeat the Empire, and Juárez returns to power. |
| **1877** | Porfirio Díaz seizes power and controls the presidency for 34 years. |

**1910-1911**    Francisco Madero leads the Revolution and overthrows the government of Diaz.

**1934-1940**    Lázaro Cárdenas is president of the Republic.

**1968**    Student Movement ends when the army fires on the crowd in Tlatelolco; Agustín Yáñez, secretary of education, works to prevent further violence.

**1994**    In the southern state of Chiápas, an armed revolt causes the worst political and economic crisis in modern Mexico's history.

**2000**    Vicente Fox, the candidate for the conservative National Action Party, is elected president.

**2001**    President Fox meets with U.S. President George W. Bush to discuss a cooperative relationship between the neighboring countries.

**2002**    Latin American leaders, including Mexico's Vicente Fox, meet in Argentina for the Global Alumni Conference to discuss technological and economic issues.

**2006**    Felipe Calderón is sworn in as Mexico's president in December.

**2007**    The Museum of the Fine Arts in Mexico City honors the 100th birthday of Frida Kahlo with the first comprehensive exhibit of her paintings in Mexico. Open from mid-June through mid-August, the exhibit draws record crowds.

## GLOSSARY

| | |
|---|---|
| **Ambushed** | Attacked by surprise from a hidden location. |
| **Anarchist** | One who rebels against all forms of government. |
| **Aqueduct** | A structure for carrying flowing water. |
| **Armada** | A fleet of Spanish warships. |
| **Bureaucracy** | A system of government administration made up of nonelected officers. |
| **Cabinet** | An advisory council for a country's leader. |
| **Civil** | Having to do with citizens; a civil war is fought between citizens of the same country. |
| **Civilian** | A member of society who does not belong to the military, the police, or the fire department. |
| **Conquistadors** | The Spanish conquerors of the New World. |
| **Conservative** | Wanting to maintain things the way they are with no reforms or changes, the opposite of liberal. |
| **Democratic** | Believing that government belongs to the people. |
| **Epidemic** | A contagious disease that affects a large percentage of the population. |
| **Exile** | When a person is forced to leave his or her home. |
| **Guerilla** | Someone who fights using sabotage and surprise tactics. |
| **Liberal** | Believing in progress and the protection of human rights, the opposite of conservative. |
| **Moderate** | Sticking to the middle of the road politically (between liberals and conservatives). |
| **Modernism** | An artistic and literary style that broke away from traditional techniques. |
| **Peasants** | Common people. |
| **Progressive** | Believing in political change and social improvement through government action. |
| **Radical** | In favor of taking extreme measures to achieve political goals. |
| **Satire** | Sarcastic humor that often makes fun of social problems and those in power |

# FURTHER READING

Chávez, Alicia Hernández. *Mexico: A Brief History*. Berkeley: University of California Press, 2006.

Herrera, Hayden, et al. *Frida Kahlo*. Minneapolis: Walker Art Center, 2007.

Levy, Buddy. *Conquistador: Hernán Cortés, King Montezuma, and the Last Stand of the Aztecs*. New York: Bantam, 2008.

Lozano, Luis Martin, and Juan Coronel Rivera. *Diego Rivera: The Complete Murals*. New York: Taschen, 2008.

Foster, Lynn V. *A Brief History of Mexico*. New York: Checkmark Books, 2007.

Fox, Vicente. *Revolution of Hope: The Life, Faith, and Dreams of a Mexican President*. New York: Plume, 2008.

Fowler, Will. *Santa Anna of Mexico*. Lincoln: University of Nebraska Press, 2007.

Meyer, Michael C., et al. *The Course of Mexican History*. New York: Oxford University Press, 2002.

Williams, Colleen Madonna Flood. *The People of Mexico*. Philadelphia: Mason Crest, 2009.

# INDEX

## PICTURE CREDITS

| | | | |
|---|---|---|---|
| 2: | IMS Communications Ltd. | 41: | Bettmann/Corbis |
| 10: | Archivo Iconografico, S.A./Corbis | 42: | Bettmann/Corbis |
| 13: | Gianni Dagli Orti/Corbis | 43: | Corbis |
| 15: | (left) Hulton/Archive; (right) Michael Zabe/Art Resource, NY | 44: | Hulton/Archive |
| | | 47: | Hulton/Archive |
| 18: | Giraudon/Art Resource | 48: | Christopher Cormack/Corbis |
| 21: | Archivo Iconografico, S.A./Corbis | 50: | Bettmann/Corbis |
| 22: | Texas State Library and Archives | 53: | Archivo Iconografico, S.A./Corbis |
| 25: | Hulton/Archive | 54: | Corbis |
| 28: | Danny Lehman/Corbis | 57: | Hulton/Archive |
| 31: | Hulton/Archive | | |
| 32: | Corbis | Cover: | (front - left to right) Library of Congress, © 2008 Jupiterimages Corporation, Library of Congress; (back) Used under license from Shutterstock, Inc. |
| 35: | Reuters NewMedia Inc./Corbis | | |
| 38: | Jan Butchofsky-Houser/Houserstock | | |

63

## INTERNET RESOURCES

**Sor Juana Inés de la Cruz Project**
http://www.dartmouth.edu/~sorjuana

**The Virtual Diego Rivera Museum**
http://www.diegorivera.com

Publisher's Note: The websites listed on this page were active at the time of publication. The publisher is not responsible for websites that have changed their address or discontinued operation since the date of publication. The publisher reviews and updates the websites each time the book is reprinted.

## CONTRIBUTORS

**Roger E. Hernández** is the most widely syndicated columnist writing on Hispanic issues in the United States. His weekly column, distributed by King Features, appears in some 40 newspapers across the country, including the *Washington Post, Los Angeles Daily News, Dallas Morning News, Arizona Republic, Rocky Mountain News* in Denver, *El Paso Times,* and *Hartford Courant.* He is also the author of *Cubans in America,* an illustrated history of the Cuban presence in what is now the United States, from the early colonists in 16th-century Florida to today's Castro-era exiles. The book was designed to accompany a PBS documentary of the same title.

Hernández's articles and essays have been published in the *New York Times, New Jersey Monthly, Reader's Digest,* and *Vista Magazine;* he is a frequent guest on television and radio political talk shows, and often travels the country to lecture on his topic of expertise. Currently, he is teaching journalism and English composition at the New Jersey Institute of Technology in Newark, where he holds the position of writer-in-residence. He is also a member of the adjunct faculty at Rutgers University.

Hernández left Cuba with his parents at the age of nine. After living in Spain for a year, the family settled in Union City, New Jersey, where Hernández grew up. He attended Rutgers University, where he earned a BA in Journalism in 1977; after graduation, he worked in television news before moving to print journalism in 1983. He lives with his wife and two children in Upper Montclair, New Jersey.

**Anna Carew-Miller** is a freelance writer and former teacher. She lives in rural Connecticut with her husband, her daughter, and a very large cat. They enjoy hiking, backpacking, and cross-country skiing. Anna has a B.A. in English from the College of William and Mary, an M.A. in English from Yale University, and a Ph.D. in American Literature from the University of New Mexico. She has done extensive research and writing on women in literature, nature writing, and Native American literature.r